This is for you.

Courtney Jones

COLLECTIONS OF A FILTHY HEART

AUSTIN MACAULEY PUBLISHERS™
LONDON * CAMBRIDGE * NEW YORK * SHARJAH

Copyright © Courtney Jones 2024

All rights reserved. No part of this publication may be reproduced, distributed, or transmitted in any form or by any means, including photocopying, recording, or other electronic or mechanical methods, without the prior written permission of the publisher, except in the case of brief quotations embodied in critical reviews and certain other noncommercial uses permitted by copyright law. For permission requests, write to the publisher.

Any person who commits any unauthorized act in relation to this publication may be liable to criminal prosecution and civil claims for damages.

Ordering Information
Quantity sales: Special discounts are available on quantity purchases by corporations, associations, and others. For details, contact the publisher at the address below.

Publisher's Cataloging-in-Publication data
Jones, Courtney
Collections of a Filthy Heart

ISBN 9781645757900 (Paperback)
ISBN 9781645757917 (Hardback)
ISBN 9781645757924 (ePub e-book)

Library of Congress Control Number: 2023913769

www.austinmacauley.com/us

First Published 2024
Austin Macauley Publishers LLC
40 Wall Street, 33rd Floor, Suite 3302
New York, NY 10005
USA

mail-usa@austinmacauley.com
+1 (646) 5125767

It was like when you accidentally slice your finger
with a knife.
For that split second, there is no pain,
yet it builds in an instant.
Incredulously.
By surprise.

And you catch your breath.

Because that tingle ripples through your insides.
And you recognize it
when open flesh meets the air.
The moment when you feel the pain.

Tears kiss your face
as the first drop of blood
meets the pad of your finger—

That's what it felt like when my heart broke for the first time.

Stumbling isn't falling, you know—

Not if you stand up stronger
than before your knees went weak.

I can still feel them,
those scars only we can see.
And maybe,
just maybe
one day we'll trace them together
and laugh at how young we were.

It wasn't the fire in her that was dangerous
or what kept people from getting close.
It was because she was made of the earth.
And it was in every breath she took,
and in every breath she let out
that stirred embers from their ash,
and it was frightening for some
to burn again.

I watched him come back
a little more each time.
And I thought to myself,
how beautiful it is
to see someone
find themselves again.

For Tim

And I'll keep you there.

Safe.

In that special place in my heart
where I never thought to have you
let alone keep you.
But there you'll be all the same.

I think you would have liked that.

I've never given my all to anyone.

    Not really.

    But—

It's not that some didn't deserve it.

    It's just—

What would I have left for myself?

For Mikey

My cousin with the beautiful eyes
lived life wild and free and with a smile on his
face.
Winking at the world.

Time.
It really is ageless
isn't it?

There's a magic in some moments.

The kind that makes a minute seem to last forever.

It's one of those days, kid...
To drink whiskey in the rain.

Ah, life!
You're complicated and painful and ugly wrapped in

pretty things.
You're mean and funny and so curiously bizarre—

But I still love you anyway
you fickle bitch.

You weren't home.
But it was nice to stay
for a while.

Promises.

They're like a sunrise, aren't they?

Beautiful.

Fleeting.

And happen every day.

Everyone comes and goes.
Some may stay,
but really—

Everyone comes and goes.

Some will have within themselves what we've lost
along the way.
Others will try to piece us back together with
their outside corners first.
And then there are the ones who take and keep the
parts of us we never meant to give away…

And when they come and whether they go—

It's our pieces that matter.
Not the people.

Some of those pieces may always be missing,
others may never fit like they used to.
And we may never find the right way to hold them in
place again anyway.

But darling,
just know—

The little pieces,
they'll always belong to you.

No matter where they are.

And after it all,
the only thing you ever understood
was that you will never
figure her out.

She was beautifully complicated,
made of all those things others couldn't piece
together.
But all she ever wanted was to understand why she
didn't want to make the pieces fit...
and make sense of a world that told her that she
should.

She kept it all so close,
hugging her secrets
like
the night cradled
the stars.

It's not that I didn't want you.

I adored you as much and as hard as I knew how.
It's that you deserved better.

And I knew enough about love to let you go.

The world doesn't forget about girls like you, doll.

They can try—

But you were made to be remembered.

And I'll think of you
when I'm dreaming wide awake.

When my eyes are open
but my heart is far away.

And I'll think of you
even though you don't want me to.

When the world is full of color
but all I feel is blue.

It's funny, isn't it?

How we create
the most beautiful things
when we're sad.

It was always there,

the secret part of her that whispered, "No" the moment she bound her heart to the man who would only break it.

And when he did, the pieces filled the sky like a thousand glittering stars—

And the moon envied their light.

Yet it was then, among the other twinkling masses of shattered goodbyes that they whispered, "It will be okay."

And it was.

And maybe you'll always run.

But maybe running isn't running away.

Maybe it's merely a head start to get to where you need to be—

And maybe it's okay...

to figure it out when you get there.

We were magic
and mayhem
and everything they said we shouldn't be.

You were my favorite hurricane,
and I was your favorite way to be swept away.

Oh silly girl,
don't apologize for feeling.

Sometimes it's OK to hide yourself from the world
because it hurts too much to try and understand it.
It's ok to suffer for its sufferings or cry from its sorrows.
Your tears can sometimes be water under someone else's bridge.

Yet, sometimes you have to be selfish.
Don't hide away from yourself because that too hurts too much to understand.

Don't apologize for being a little scared to seek solace from the shadows that hide inside and chase us all.

Don't apologize—

Not for any of it.
And not to anyone.

Because, you silly girl,

as long as you feel something,
you'll be okay.

You're half my mind.

You're all my madness.

But love,
don't you know moments are fleeting
and forever is so far away?

Don't you know that people break
and everyone aches
and perfect is for the naïve?

But, also—

Don't you think there's a place
in between promises and moving lips
where everything's what it seems?

I do.

Oh darling girl,
just learn to love yourself.
Because once you do, you'll love the world.

And you'll set it on fucking fire.

You weren't my first.

And I wasn't your last.

But for a moment we had it,
if only for just a little while.

When I'm old and gray and tired
and when I'm wrinkled and spotted with age,
when my tattoos fade, stretched with the years...
my skin ravaged by time...

And when my body is brittle, but my heart is young,
when my bones don't move like they used to:

They will ask me if I have lived.

And I will say yes.
I lived wild and free and with abandon.
And I'll tell them to love hard and laugh loud and to
spin around in the rain.

Because living is meant for us all.

Find the silver lining
always.
Find it
and paint your own sky.

She smiled, he thought,
in a way that
brought rainbows
out at night.

Darling,
let's pretend

we can see the wind,
and let it carry us away.

We have plenty
of ways to fall, my dear,
just catch me
and we'll spiral together.

I cannot gift you with a bouquet of flowers,
but you may have my bones to bury.
And over the years
beneath the soil,
there they'll stay—

With handfuls of daffodils that bloom
just for you.

You know—

Sometimes we see better with our eyes closed.

Deep down, where no one else can see,
I'm just a girl.

And even deeper, where I haven't even touched yet,
I'm also just me.

That's the place where we should meet.
Maybe we'll both get there.

And maybe one day if we meet again, things will be different.
Maybe I'll be different.
Maybe you'll be different.
Maybe we'll both be strangers.

And maybe it will be good to start again.

I can't apologize.

I broke my own heart
long before
I broke yours.

It's 2 a.m.

and this moment is for us.

For the ones who feel most alive when peace of mind
dies in our bones
and a wild brilliance grips our brains.

It's 2 a.m.

and 10,000 thoughts explode at once,
like 10,000 birds are taking flight.

It's 2 a.m.

and this moment is ours.
The ones who would rather live with 10,000 birds in
our heads
than exist without ever having left the ground.

I love 2 a.m.

I adore you.
You're poetry

and magic
and trouble
and sin.

You know I adore you.
But I'm wild

and lost
and trouble
and sin.

It's not their fault

but

they'll hurt you without knowing it,

every time—

The beautiful ones.

She felt naked. And alone,
like a tree stripped bare of its leaves in winter.
Yet, all she ever wanted was to feel warmth.
And burn with the fire that consumed her.

Maybe we're meant to feel the kind of pain that
never leaves.
Maybe it's because the wounds are supposed to
remind us that what we endure is beautiful.
And maybe that should be enough
to let someone trace your scars.

Sometimes, it doesn't exist—

Time.

Because you think some moments will last forever.

But then it hits

and it hurts.

And you realize the only time you're ever on time is

when it's too late.

There are no more moments—

Other than the memories that made you wish time existed if only to stand still.

And who knows, no one really.
Maybe we're not supposed to.
Maybe figuring it out means finally realizing
we know nothing at all.

Darling,
if you could see yourself the way I do,
you would never close your eyes.

No matter who she woke up to,
she was always thinking of someone else.
Maybe because she hadn't found him yet,
or maybe because she hasn't found herself.

Before the day decides you're ugly

just know,
when you're kind—

You're beautiful.

The worst ache
about heartbreak
is when it feels like home.
Cheating eyes,
alibi lullabies,
silly girl, it's time to go.

But hopeful hearts die bleeding slow.

I wonder
If one day I'll look back on these ones
when I would sit alone
with a bottle of wine and a head full of thoughts...

And wonder
If I'll ever never be alone again,

but then—

I wonder

If I'm ever the center of someone else,
will I miss the solitude of myself?

Loving him
was like visiting a fortune teller.
And regretting it.

She didn't come with strings attached

    because she was a puppet.
    She was just made
    to be the type of girl
    you didn't want to let go.

Pretty doll on the shelf.
Take her down,
pass her around.
Feel better about yourself.

I'm pretty fucking mad.

Pissed off you exist.
If I had a hit list,
your name would be the next one on it.
Dateline. No witnesses.

But its cathartic—

To write words
when your heart hurts,
and the pen stains the page.

It's like the ink

tattoos what you think,
but your body still reports to a mind
that's trapped in a cage.

Eh, babe?

Lord knows I'm no Adele.
I don't want to meet someone like you
or wish you well—
I hope you dwell in that empty shell

of entitlement
I almost fell into with you.

I didn't deserve what you did to me.

The way you treated me
unapologetically and repeatedly—

Accountability, though
can't be taken by proxy.

Eh, babe?

You helped me find her, you know—

That version of myself
who never would have
given you a chance.

He was beautiful.
But he was beautiful in the type of way a panther stalked its prey.

Sleek. Deliberate. Silent.

He was the type of beautiful you knew would be your death.
Yet, you welcomed the slaughter anyway.

She looked at him just then—

And was lost.

His eyes held secrets like fire cradles heat.

He was the type of man others would follow into hell.

And she would have went with him, too.

If only he had asked.

But out of all my lovers, sir—

I know that you were the only one
who really loved me.

They may say that you're ridiculous in a million different ways.
I say that I love the million different ways that you're ridiculous.

Some will break you.
Some will break you so fucking hard
they'll have you thinking you broke yourself.

Fuck them.

It happens all the time, you know.
Anything.

He isn't going to be the one—

That guy who's supposed to save you from yourself.

I would love you for a 1000 years
if I only had the chance.
And you would fall in love with me again
if you gave me a second one.

A crimson kiss.
Her lips—
Hold something
so beautiful.

It's a lonely place,

that look on his face—

When he's not looking at you.

It's a slow, agonizing death
isn't it?
To be murdered by mirrors.

How painful it must be
to be cut each day
by a reflection wielding
broken shards of glass.

And what a pity it is
when bones are beautiful
in the eyes of their own beholder.

Yes—

What a slow, agonizing death it must be.
To be murdered by mirrors.

Home.
I guess it really just is
where all the odds and ends
make you feel whole.
Isn't it?

He was a thief.

Of her thoughts
her mind
her heart.

Slow and quick
tiny nicks.

All at once
always
a hundred times.

Yes,
he was a thief.

And she was his
paper cut masterpiece.

That was something she never understood:
Why she was always in
someone else's arms
when his hug felt like home.

He knew she was wild,
and he always tried to save what he couldn't

understand—

Like she was some broken thing that needed fixing.
And when she left,
he couldn't help but wonder

how far she flew away.

I'll always love you

in between the seconds—

That place where I heard my own heartbeat.

Let's dance

barefoot in the kitchen
to the music
our parents used to listen to.

And he knew deep down
in his sensible soul
that he always needed
just a little of her crazy.

He caressed her skin
inch by inch
goosebumps trailing his fingertips.

Her body came alive
with every move
and every stroke.

Her senses were lost.
Yet in all the ways she felt his hands,
he could never touch her heart.

She didn't even

know it was hers—

That type of beauty
not even an artist could paint.

Girls with messy hearts
will drive you wild
and leave you free.

And it was a wild thing.
When she took back
what he thought
he was entitled to keep.

I think

I'll always

choose madness.

It's where the magic happens.

It was in her voice.

She was a woman who laughed
and cried
and smoked
and drank,
who dreamed
and dared
and tried
and failed.

And she lived in the clouds
while sturdy legs
held onto the earth.

And you couldn't help

but listen
when she spoke.

It's dark tonight

and cold outside

and the snow is gently falling.

And I can't help but wonder

how many lovers

are keeping warm while I'm alone.

Dark

cold

gently falling.

I whispered the words
that you sang to her.

He said
she smelled of summer
and every memory he wanted to make.
And then
he turned his back
with the color of the leaves.

She was
far from a
gentle lover.

But she held onto
every moment.

Until the moment
she pushed him away.

Buried bones
and broken hearts
both
keep their secrets.

But darling,
didn't you know?

She was yours
before you ever met.

The night
was simply waiting
for the stars to light the way.

She
tangled up
his heart

like he
tangled up
her hair.

Please know:

When you buy her flowers,
she may sometimes forget them
once they wilt and the petals fall.

But always,
please know:

She will forever remember
how their scent first filled the air.

Like the feeling of a love that lasts
long after youth loses its bloom.

You know what, sir?
You're just

as odd and wonderful to me
as breakfast for dinner.

"Don't mind us,"

she said.

"We're a little drunk

and a lot in love."

I promise to always
write you handwritten notes.
And I promise
to still love the wine stains
you leave on them.

She smiled,
and it was then he knew
that he would spend forever
trying to kiss
the secrets from her lips.

He was
a teasing breath
to a girl gasping for air.

She was in the wind
and he felt her lips
every time
the breeze touched his skin.

To a weathered soul,
his kiss was like sunshine
streaming through a windowpane.

His eyes were the color
of liquid amber.
And she was drunk
off his cognac gaze.

For all the words I never say—

    The ones I write
    will always be
    for you.

A girl's relationship with loving herself

is an adventure that's

far greater

far wilder

than any romance.

Lovers aren't meant to last.
Lovers are made for memories.
Their pleasure is art, their taste is insatiable.
Theirs is a scent that lingers with secrets.
Lovers are meant for loss,
but they are made to be remembered.

It's both my greatest fear

and greatest love:
The blank page.